Planning the Catholic Funeral

Terence P. Curley

LITURGICAL PRESS
Collegeville, Minnesota

www.litpress.org

*In memory of my mother
Eileen C. Curley,
may she experience the peace of God's kingdom.*

Cover design by Ann Blattner

Excerpts from the English translation of the *Rite of Baptism for Children* © 1969, International Committee on English in the Liturgy, Inc. (ICEL); excerpts from the *Order of Christian Funerals* © 1985, ICEL. All rights reserved.

Excerpts from the *Lectionary for Mass for Use in the Dioceses of the United States of America* copyright © 1970, 1986, 1992, 1998, 2001, Confraternity of Christian Doctrine, Inc., Washington, D.C. All rights reserved. No part of the Lectionary for Mass may be reproduced by any means without permission in writing from the copyright owner.

Excerpt from the Pastoral Introduction to the Appendix of the *Order of Christian Funerals:* "Cremation," copyright © 1997, United States Catholic Conference, Inc. (presently: United States Conference of Catholic Bishops), 3211 Fourth Street, N.E., Washington, D.C., 20017, is reproduced with permission by license of the copyright owner. All rights reserved.

Scripture texts in this work are taken from the *New American Bible with Revised New Testament and Revised Psalms* © 1991, 1986, 1970, Confraternity of Christian Doctrine, Washington, D.C., and are used by permission of the copyright owner. All rights reserved. No part of the *New American Bible* may be reproduced in any form without permission in writing from the copyright owner.

© 2005 by the Order of Saint Benedict, Collegeville, Minnesota. All rights reserved. No part of this book may be reproduced in any form, by print, microfilm, microfiche, mechanical recording, photocopying, translation, or by any other means, known or yet unknown, for any purpose except brief quotations in reviews, without the previous written permission of the Liturgical Press, Saint John's Abbey, P.O. Box 7500, Collegeville, Minnesota 56321-7500. Printed in the United States of America.

1   2   3   4   5   6   7   8

Cataloging-in-Publication Data

Curley, Terence P., 1944–
    Planning the Catholic funeral / Terence P. Curley.
        p. cm.
    Summary: "A guide to plan Catholic funeral rites, on short notice or in advance of death, according to the Order of Christian Funerals"—Provided by publisher.
    Includes bibliographical references.
    ISBN-13: 978-0-8146-1524-9 (pbk. : alk. paper)
    ISBN-10: 0-8146-1524-4 (pbk. : alk. paper)
    1. Funeral service—Catholic Church. 2. Catholic Church. Order of Christian funerals. I. Title.

BX2035.6.F853C87 2005
264'.020985—dc22   2004025217

Contents

A Blessing   iv

Preface   1

Principal Data and Decisions

1. Funeral Home and Parish   2
   Information about the Deceased   2
2. Committal and Disposition of the Body of the Deceased   5
3. Scheduling the Principal Funeral Liturgy   6
4. Scheduling the Funeral Vigil   7
5. Visitation   7

Liturgical and Liturgically Related Decisions

6. Leaders/Presiders   9
7. Funeral Vigil   9
8. Pallbearers   11
9. Placing of the Pall   11
10. Placing of Christian Symbols   12
11. Server(s)   13
12. Lector(s)   13
13. Readings   15
14. Homilies   16
15. Prayer of the Faithful   17
16. Preparation of the Gifts at Mass   18
17. Ministers of Holy Communion   18
18. Music   19
19. Remembrance of the Deceased   20
20. Rite of Committal   21
21. Memorabilia   22
22. Gathering in the Presence of the Body   23
23. Transfer of the Body to the Church
    or to the Place of Committal   23
24. Refreshments and Luncheon   24

Conclusion   24

Prayers   25

Appendices

Appendix 1: Options for the Funeral Vigil   26
Appendix 2: Options for Funeral and Rite of Committal   27
Appendix 3: Scripture Selection Guide   28
Appendix 4: Music List   34
Appendix 5: Giving a Remembrance of the Deceased   35
Summary of Requests and Information   36

A Blessing

May the love of God and the peace of the Lord Jesus Christ
bless and console us
and gently wipe every tear from your eyes:
in the name of the Father, and of the Son, and of the Holy Spirit.

Amen.[1]

---

[1] From the *Order of Christian Funerals,* §223. This booklet tries to take into account many circumstances. There are elements considered here that many not be relevant to every funeral, and also, this booklet does not exhaust every possibility offered by the full edition of the *Order of Christian Funerals,* which takes into account many special circumstances. Those responsible for funeral planning on a regular basis are encouraged to be thoroughly familiar with the *Order of Christian Funerals (OCF)* and its appendix, "Cremation" *(OCFc).* The *Order of Christian Funerals* (1989), approved for use in the dioceses of the United States of America by the National Conference of Catholic Bishops (now the United States Conference of Catholic Bishops), is widely available for purchase, including from the Liturgical Press (Collegeville, Minnesota). The appendix on "Cremation," published in 1997, is available separately. At the Liturgical Press, the appendix is now included with purchases of the *Order of Christian Funerals.* These works are abbreviated here as *OCF* (the full Order) and *OCFc* (appendix on cremation).

Other bereavement titles are available through Liturgical Press, ph. 1-800-858-5450. The author also has works on this subject available through Andrew Lane Company, ph. 1-800-451-2520.

Preface

If you have recently experienced the death of a loved one, please know that the Church shares your grief and wishes to convey hope. Whenever Mass is celebrated—a celebration of the saving work of Christ—the Mass is offered for both the deceased and the living. The Church also prays for the deceased and the living in the Liturgy of the Hours, prayed by many lay persons, religious, and clergy throughout the world. You have the support and prayers of the believing community in your own parish and throughout the world.

Ever since the earliest days of the Church, bereaved families, close friends, and parts of the larger community have gathered together, ritually, to support each other, share grief, and express hope in the resurrection of loved ones, based on our hope in Christ.

This booklet is written both for those who are planning a funeral on short notice and for those who want to plan a funeral far in advance of death. As a "guide" this booklet leads you through the funeral planning process, especially the journeys of ritual. This booklet also serves as a record of memories: it is not only a historical record for posterity, but it is also a tool that can be used in the natural human process of grieving.

In the case of a recent death, a member of the funeral home staff or parish staff or both will be more than willing to help you complete the forms in this booklet. No one wants you to feel more overwhelmed at a time of loss than you may already feel.

This booklet is arranged so that you can work your way through the planning process by filling in the blanks. The summary offers an opportunity for you and those helping you to have an overview of your decisions. When completed, the summary can be copied or removed.

This book is meant to help you. May God's compassionate love strengthen you and those you love during this time of profound preparation—and in the days to come.

1. Funeral Home and Parish

The death of a loved one leaves many decisions for those who remain, especially the family of the deceased. Staff members of the parish and the funeral home are available to assist you through the funeral planning process, through the rites themselves, and afterwards.

> I / We would like this funeral home to handle the funeral arrangements:
>
> _____
>
> I / We would like this parish church to handle the liturgical arrangements for the funeral:
>
> _____

Information about the Deceased

Depending upon circumstances, you may wish to return to this information form after scheduling the liturgies and visitations times in sections 2–6, below.

The information in this section will be of help to both the parish and funeral home staffs, who use this information in a variety of ways (announcements, informing newspapers, composing remembrance cards, etc.). The next form is repeated on pages 43–44, in the summary.

A homilist and/or anyone giving a remembrance of the deceased (see sections 14 and 19, below) will also find this information helpful.

Name of the deceased: _____

Nickname: _____

Name to be used in liturgical prayers: _____

_____

Maiden name: _____

Age of the deceased: _____

Son/Daughter of: _____

_____

Surviving loved ones:

    Spouse: _____

    Children (names, places of residence, spouses): _____

    _____

    _____

    _____

    _____

    _____

    Grandchildren and great-grandchildren (names): _____

    _____

    _____

    _____

    _____

    Others of special note: _____

    _____

    _____

Place of birth: _____

Name of spouse (if deceased): _____

Date and place of marriage: _____

Residence history: _____

_____

_____

Education history: _____
_____
_____
_____

Work history: _____
_____
_____
_____

Special or ordinary accomplishments: _____
_____
_____
_____

Parish membership and service: _____
_____
_____

Membership in other organizations: _____
_____
_____
_____

Hobbies and recreational activities: _____
_____
_____
_____

Words or descriptions that characterized the deceased: ___
_____
_____
_____

Preceded in death by: _____
_____

2. Committal and Disposition of the Body of the Deceased

I / We would like:

_____ a traditional burial.

At this cemetery: _____
_____
_____

On this date: _____

At this time: _____

_____ cremation[2] to occur before the funeral liturgy.

_____ cremation to occur after the funeral liturgy.

I / We would like the committal of the ashes to take place:

At this place: _____
_____

On this date: _____

At this time: _____

Special circumstances: _____
_____
_____
_____
_____
_____

Typically, burial soon follows the funeral, but circumstances may prevent this.

---

[2] "The cremated remains of a body should be treated with the same respect given to the human body from which they come. This includes the use of a worthy vessel to contain the ashes, the manner in which they are carried, the care and attention to appropriate placement and transport, and the final disposition. The cremated remains should be buried in a grave or entombed in a mausoleum or columbarium. The practices of scattering cremated remains on the sea, from the air, or on the ground, or keeping cremated remains in the home of a relative or friend of the deceased are not the reverent disposition that the Church requires. Whenever possible, appropriate means for recording with dignity the memory of the deceased should be adopted, such as a plaque or stone which records the name of the deceased" (*OCFc* §417).

3. Scheduling the Principal Funeral Liturgy

The principal funeral liturgy is usually a celebration of the Mass with its Liturgy of the Word and Liturgy of the Eucharist. We read that "In the eucharistic sacrifice, the Church's celebration of Christ's Passover from death to life, the faith of the baptized in the paschal mystery is renewed and nourished."[3] Nonetheless the funeral liturgy may be celebrated outside of a Mass.[4] "The funeral liturgy outside Mass is ordinarily celebrated in the parish church, but may also be celebrated in the home of the deceased, a funeral home, parlor, chapel of rest, or cemetery chapel."[5]

I / We would like:

_____ the principal funeral liturgy within the eucharistic celebration of a Mass.

    I / We would like the Mass to be celebrated

        _____ in the parish church.

        at _____, with the approval of the parish staff.

(The place might be a recognized chapel within a parish.)

I / We would like:

_____ the principal funeral liturgy to be celebrated apart from a Mass.

    I / We would like the celebration to take place at:

    _____

    I / We would like this to be:

        _____ with the distribution of Holy Communion.

        _____ without the distribution of Holy Communion.

---

[3] *OCF* §3.

[4] This latter option may be chosen because of liturgical law prohibiting a funeral Mass on certain days or because a priest is unavailable, or for pastoral reasons (*OCF* §178).

[5] *OCF* §179.

The determination of the date and time of the principal funeral liturgy helps to determine other arrangements. The scheduling of all times depends on the availability of ministers.

> I / We would like the principal funeral liturgy to take place on this day at this time:
> _____

4. Scheduling the Funeral Vigil

The funeral vigil was formerly called "the wake." In coordination with the arrangements of visitation (in the next section), and in coordination with the time of the principal funeral liturgy (considered above) it is important to determine the time of the vigil liturgy. Usually a vigil service will take place during the evening of a day when there are visitation hours. Rarely (but occasionally) a family requests a Catholic funeral without a vigil.

"The vigil may be celebrated in the home of the deceased, in the funeral home, parlor or chapel of rest, or in some other suitable place."[6] The place and date of the vigil will almost certainly be the place of (or one of the places of) visitation,[7] considered below.

> I / We would like the funeral vigil to take place:
> At this place: _____
> At this time: _____
> On this date: _____

5. Visitation

Along with the funeral vigil arrangements, certain other dates and times—as well as place(s)—need to be determined. Family members and friends will want to come together at these times to remember and grieve for the deceased and to console one another. Typically a family has some private time with the body

---

[6] *OCF* §55.
[7] "As needs require, and especially if the funeral liturgy or rite of committal is not to take place for a few days, the vigil may be celebrated more than once and should be adapted to each occasion" (*OCF* §67).

According to the *Order of Christian Funerals*, "The family and friends of the deceased should not be excluded from taking part in the services sometimes provided by undertakers, for example, preparation and laying out the body" (*OCF* §20).

before public visitation begins. It may be better to schedule more than one session of the visitation period so that the family may gather together for a meal or rest instead of attempting a marathon session of several hours. Often Catholic parishes have visitation the day before a funeral and on the day of the funeral, before the principal funeral liturgy.

Often visitations happen at the funeral home or at a parish church or chapel meaningful to the deceased. Sometimes visitations take place in a private home. Visitations can occur in a combination of places.

In preparation for the visitation, a member of the funeral home staff will ask you to select and provide clothing for the body of the deceased. You may ask the funeral home staff in what way you can take part in the preparation of the body.

I / We would like there to be public visitation on these days (or this day) and at these hours: _____

_____

_____

I / We would like there to be private visitation on this day at this time (this often precedes public visitation): _____

_____

The place(s) of visitation is (are): _____

_____

Notes concerning the clothing and the preparation of the body of the deceased: _____

_____

_____

❖

Decisions about those called upon to minister and participate in the funeral liturgies are best made in consultation with the parish and funeral home staffs. Because of their experience and their ability to answer many of your questions, conversations with these professionals will facilitate the process of planning and accomplishing what is appropriate for the funeral rituals you are planning. If you have experienced a recent loss, the funeral home staff will probably already have been of assistance to you. Now is an appropriate time to be in touch with the parish staff, if this has not yet happened. If you wish, a member of the funeral home staff will contact the parish for you.

In the *Order of Christian Funerals,* certain times constitute significant moments along the way in a prayerful journey for and with loved ones. The more familiar we are with the rituals the better we can celebrate and remember loved ones in faith-filled ways. There are opportunities when you may participate or request another person to participate in the liturgy. Planning and doing liturgical actions is essential for good liturgy and becomes a faith-filled way to remember a loved one.

> "At the funeral liturgy, the community gathers with the family and friends of the deceased to give praise and thanks to God for Christ's victory over sin and death, to commend the deceased to God's tender mercy and compassion, and to seek strength in the proclamation of the paschal mystery" (*OCF* §129).

6. Leaders/Presiders

If possible, I / we would like this (these) minister(s) to be involved in leading services:

At the vigil: _____

At the funeral liturgy: _____

At the committal: _____

_____ I / We would like the parish staff to decide the matters of who will preside when.

7. Funeral Vigil

In the early Church, Christians were seen as "people of vigilance," watching for the Lord's return in glory. They saw everything in terms of the imminent coming of the full reign of God. Death reminds us that we too know (from faith) that the reign of God that Jesus proclaimed is "at hand" (Mark 1:15) and we wait for Jesus to come again (Revelation 22:20). We are called to vigilance.

The funeral vigil is a time of prayer—in words and silence—for the deceased Christian and for those who have experienced loss in the death.

The *Order of Christian Funerals* provides that the vigil service may follow a "vigil-rite" format or a format more akin to the traditional evening prayer of the Church from its Liturgy of the Hours. In either case, this rite may include the "reception of the body" in the parish church. In appendix 1 of this booklet, there are outlines of the various options for the funeral vigil. If the parish does not customarily follow a single option—or if a particular option in the appendix is attractive to you—please discuss the options available with a parish staff member.

> _____ I / We would like to do what is customary in regard to the format of the funeral vigil.
>
> _____ I / We would like to discuss the format options for the funeral vigil with a parish staff member.

It is best to discuss with a parish staff member when the "reception of the body" will take place for a funeral where a body is present. In Catholic parishes this has typically taken place at the beginning of a funeral Mass or at the beginning of a funeral liturgy outside Mass. However, with funeral vigils now often taking place in parish churches, the rite of reception is also taking place at the vigil. Either way is a valid option, but once a body has been "received" the coffin remains closed.

> I / We would like the reception of the body to take place:
>
> _____ at the funeral vigil.
>
> _____ at the funeral Mass or liturgy.
>
> _____ I / We would like the parish staff to decide the matter of when the body is to be received.

In addition to the liturgical rites of the Church many Catholics find comfort in praying the rosary. You may or may not wish to have a rosary prayed publicly during the visitation period, before or after the vigil liturgy. A parish society to which the deceased person belonged may wish to lead the rosary.

> _____ I / We would like to have the rosary prayed publicly during the time of visitation, and I/we would like the rosary to be led by _____ at this time _____ on this day_____
>
> _____ I / We would prefer not to have the rosary prayed publicly during the time of visitation.
>
> _____ I / We would like the parish staff to decide the matter of praying the rosary or not.

8. Pallbearers

Traditionally, serving as a pallbearer has been a way for persons especially close to the deceased to both participate in a special way in the funeral and to perform the useful function of carrying the coffin. Sometimes there are two groups of pallbearers: a group that actually helps carry the coffin and an honorary group (for example, members of a parish society to which the deceased person belonged). When choosing pallbearers it is good to consult with the funeral home staff to determine the physical demands of being a pallbearer for this particular funeral.

I / We would like the following persons to be pallbearers for the funeral: _____

_____

_____

_____

_____

_____

_____ I / We would like the parish staff to decide the matter of who the pallbearers will be.

In the Letter to the Colossians we read "You were buried with [Christ] in baptism, in which you were also raised with him through faith in the power of God, who raised him from the dead" (2:12).

9. Placing of the Pall

When the family and friends of the deceased come together for the liturgy in the gathering area of the worship space there is the placing of a large white cloth known as the funeral pall.[8] Technically this rite is optional, but its rich symbolism has made its use practically universal in Catholic funeral liturgy in the United States. The placing of the pall often takes place at the beginning of the principal funeral liturgy, but it could also take place at the funeral vigil.[9] The pall is a reminder of the white garment in which the deceased was clothed at baptism.

To place a pall over a coffin requires at least two persons. This can be done by the presider and a server (or assistant), but ideally, family members or friends are selected to place the pall.

"See in this white garment the outward sign of your Christian dignity. With your family and friends to help you by word and example, bring that dignity unstained into the everlasting life of heaven" (*Rite of Baptism for Children*, §63).

---

[8] *OCF* §133.
[9] *OCF* §§58 and 133.

Good candidates for placing the pall are those who were helpful to the deceased in living the Christian faith.

> The family designates the following people for the unfolding and placing of the pall on the coffin at the entrance of the church: _____
>
> _____
>
> _____ I / We would like the parish staff to decide the matter of who will place the pall.

10. Placing of Christian Symbols

The opening rituals in the principal funeral liturgy symbolize the return of the baptized to the place of beginnings and endings. For the principal liturgy, a family may (optionally) choose certain other symbols, in addition to the pall, to be placed on the coffin. This symbol might be a Book of the Gospels or Bible, a crucifix, a rosary, or another meaningful religious object.[10] An object that was owned and used by the deceased person is most appropriate for placement on the coffin. According to the *Order of Christian Funerals,* "If in this rite a symbol of the Christian life is to be placed on the coffin, it is carried in the procession and is placed on the coffin by a family member, friend, or minister at the conclusion of the procession."[11]

Before the principal liturgy and before the coffin is closed, family members may wish to place personal remembrances (not of high monetary value) in the coffin.

> We would like to place the following Christian symbol(s) on the coffin: _____
>
> _____
>
> The person(s) designated to place the Christian symbol(s) is (are): _____
>
> _____
>
> _____ I / We do not wish to place an additional Christian symbol on the coffin.
>
> _____ I / We would like the parish staff to decide the matter of additional Christian symbols.

---

[10] See *OCF* §§163 and 188.
[11] *OCF* §134.

12   *Liturgical and Liturgically Related Decisions*

11. Server(s)

Many parishes have adult servers or acolytes to assist at funeral liturgies. Youth continue to be servers also. It is important that servers have received Mass-serving instruction if the funeral liturgy is a Mass. This is especially important for visiting servers from a parish other than the one where the funeral is to be celebrated. Often family members (such as grandchildren) are invited to serve. When asking a family member or a friend of the family to serve, please be certain that the person has been trained for this ministry (especially for Mass) or is comfortable with what will be required (such as assisting a minister at the funeral vigil). When a server is from another parish, the parish staff should be consulted so that a staff member (or the presider) can help instruct the visiting server in regard to any local particularities.

> I / We request that the following person(s) be server(s) for the funeral vigil: _____
>
> _____
>
> I / We request that the following person(s) be server(s) for the principal funeral liturgy: _____
>
> _____
>
> _____ I / We would like the parish staff to decide the matter of who the servers will be.

12. Lector(s)

The lector has a special role in Catholic liturgy. The proclaiming of the Word of God is a symbol of God's presence in the believing community. This action goes far beyond merely reading. Proclaiming the Word, especially during the funeral journey, is an act of faith and trust in "the God of all consolation."[12]

Lectors for the vigil and for the funeral liturgy proper (Mass or outside Mass) may be selected by family members, in consultation with the parish staff.

In determining who will be reading at a funeral and funeral vigil, it is helpful to coordinate with a parish staff member the

---
[12] *OCF* §342.

number and selections of readings that are to be used (see section 13 and appendix 3). Often only one lector is needed for a funeral vigil, though a second lector might proclaim the responsorial psalm—though preferably that is sung.[13] (Typically a funeral vigil has one reading in addition to the Gospel, though an additional, nonscriptural reading can also be chosen when the Liturgy of the Hours is celebrated.)

One or two readings may precede the proclamation of the Gospel at the principal funeral liturgy.[14] When two readings precede the Gospel there may be two lectors, in which case the first lector proclaims the reading from the Old Testament (or, in the Easter Season, from the Acts of the Apostles or Revelation),[15] and the second lector proclaims from the New Testament. Having a different reader for each reading is encouraged in the introduction to the *Lectionary for Mass* (§52). Whether there is one lector or two, a responsorial psalm, preferably sung, follows the first reading.[16]

Many dioceses and parishes have liturgical guidelines to assist you in selecting lectors. They may specify that (a) the lector be a person strong in faith, (b) the lector has the requisite skills to read and proclaim, and/or (c) special allowance (outside of Mass) be given for interfaith/ecumenical participation according to Church norms and guidelines.

> For pastoral reasons and if circumstances allow, a nonbiblical reading may be included at morning or evening prayer in addition to the reading from Scripture, as is the practice in the office of readings (*OCF* §360).

> The Gospel is typically proclaimed by a deacon or priest, but when neither is available, a lay minister presides and proclaims the Gospel at the funeral vigil (*OCF* §14).

I / We request that the following person(s) be lector(s) for the funeral vigil:

For the first reading: _____

For the responsorial psalm or responsory (if not sung): _____
_____

For the second reading (if there is one): _____

The Gospel is to be read by: _____

_____ I / We would like the parish staff to decide the matter of who the lectors will be at the funeral vigil.

---

[13] *OCF* §26.
[14] *OCF* §138.
[15] *OCF* §345.
[16] *OCF* §139.

> I / We request that the following person(s) be lector(s) for the principal funeral liturgy:
>
> For the first reading: _____
>
> For the responsorial psalm (if not sung): _____
>
> _____
>
> For the second reading (if there is one): _____
>
> _____
>
> The Gospel is to be read by: _____
>
> _____
>
> _____ I / We would like the parish staff to decide the matter of who the readers will be at the principal funeral liturgy.

The Gospel is typically proclaimed by a deacon or priest, but when neither is available, a lay minister presides and proclaims the Gospel at the funeral liturgy outside Mass (OCF §14).

13. Readings

You may be invited to select Scripture readings for the funeral vigil and for the principal funeral liturgy. As noted above, the number of readings at the funeral vigil and the principal funeral liturgy may vary. The principal funeral liturgy may have one or two readings before the Gospel. In appendix 3 you can find a list of Scripture readings from the *Order of Christian Funerals*.

> We request that the following readings be proclaimed at the funeral vigil:
>
> The first reading: _____
>
> The responsorial psalm or responsory (if not sung): _____
>
> _____
>
> The second reading (if there is one): _____
>
> The Gospel: _____
>
> _____ I / We would like the parish staff to decide the matter of readings for the funeral vigil.

> I / We request that the following readings be proclaimed at the principal funeral liturgy:
>
> The first reading: _____
>
> The responsorial psalm (if not sung): _____
>
> The second reading (if there is one): _____
>
> The Gospel: _____
>
> _____ I / We would like the parish staff to decide the matter of readings for the principal funeral liturgy.

14. Homilies

You can anticipate that there will be a homily at the funeral vigil and at the principal funeral liturgy.[17] These homilies are meant to be based upon the Scripture readings which are proclaimed during the rites. The deceased may well be mentioned. This, however, is done within the context of God's love and the mystery of Christ's life, death, and resurrection. It is not meant to be a eulogy, which only acknowledges human actions. Rather, a homily proclaims a Christian message: what God has accomplished in the world—and in the funeral rites this can include what God has accomplished in and through the deceased. It is God alone who brings to fruition the good work begun in baptism (see Philippians 1:6).

Information of interest to a homilist may include stories or descriptions that characterize the deceased. For example, "Every Sunday morning, after Mass, Louise/Louis would always gather the family together for a meal. She/He often explained that the previous generation had done the same during the old days when people fasted from midnight before going to Mass, intending to receive Communion." It could be helpful to the homilist(s) if you gave examples of how you saw the deceased living the Gospel.

You may wish to record information (in addition to what is on the forms at the beginning and end of this booklet) on a separate sheet of paper to be given to the homilist(s) and anyone sharing a remembrance of the deceased (see section 19). You may wish to simply copy what you have recorded and have a funeral or parish staff member give it to the appropriate person(s). If you have

---

[17] *OCF* §§ 61, 166, 192, 361. In regard to funeral vigils, the *Order of Christian Funerals*, when considered with the *General Instruction of the Liturgy of the Hours*, §47, indicates that the homily is optional only in the case of the use of evening prayer.

already completed the "Information about the Deceased" form, you may have already recorded sufficient information. You may wish to return to that form at this time. (The form is on pages 3–4 and repeated on pages 43–44 in the back of this booklet.)

15. Prayer of the Faithful

The *Order of Christian Funerals* provides sample prayers for the petitions, but new intercessions may be composed.[18] These prayers or petitions are a way of seeking God's help and assistance for all people. These prayers may be adapted to the assembly's circumstances and needs, perhaps mentioning other family members or close friends who have died. A parish staff person may offer to help you write the intercessions, or you may simply make it known that you would like certain persons or concerns mentioned in these prayers.

I / We would like to have the names of the following deceased persons and the following concerns to be mentioned in prayer as part of the intercessions of the funeral liturgy: _____

_____
_____
_____
_____
_____
_____

_____ I / We would like the parish staff to decide the matter of the content of the intercessions.

For the principal funeral liturgy, you may request that an experienced reader whom you know (perhaps someone already chosen as a lector, above) proclaim these prayers. Occasionally it is desired that more than one person read the intercessions. Up to two persons would respect a certain consistency and minimal movement in this liturgical setting and prayer time. In this case,

---

[18] See *OCF* §29. The *Order of Christian Funerals* calls these prayers "General Intercessions" but the expression in the *General Instruction of the Roman Missal* (2002) is "Prayer of the Faithful."

Prayer of the Faithful 17

dividing the intercessions into the first several petitions (proclaimed by one reader) and the last several petitions (proclaimed by a second reader) seems to work better than alternating the reader after each petition.

> I / We request that the following person proclaim the intercessions at the principal funeral liturgy:
>
> _____
>
> _____ I / We would like the parish staff to decide the matter of who is to proclaim the intercessions.

16. Preparation of the Gifts at Mass

When a funeral Mass is celebrated, you are encouraged to select family members or friends to bring the gifts of bread and wine forward.[19] This happens after the intercessions have concluded, at the beginning of the Liturgy of the Eucharist. Sometimes other people accompany the gift bearers, even though they do not actually carry the bread and wine.

> I / We request that the following persons bring the gifts forward:
>
> _____
>
> _____

17. Ministers of Holy Communion

At the time of a funeral, there will sometimes be visiting priests or deacons, and often there will be extraordinary ministers of Holy Communion—from within or outside the parish—who can assist in the distribution of the consecrated bread and wine, the Body and Blood of Christ, during a funeral Mass or communion service as part of the funeral liturgy. In addition to any visiting clergy, there is naturally a desire to invite friends and family to serve as ministers of Holy Communion. It is important that persons chosen for this ministry both have some experience distributing the Eucharist and be comfortable ministering at this particular funeral.

---

[19] *OCF* §144.

> I / We would like the following person(s) to assist in the distribution of Holy Communion:
>
> _____
>
> _____
>
> _____ I / We would like the parish staff to decide the matter of who is to distribute Holy Communion.

18. Music

The selection of liturgical music is very important for worship during the funeral rites. Music may be selected for use at the vigil and for the principal funeral liturgy (for Mass or outside Mass). A listing of sacred song is provided in appendix 4—though the possibilities for hymnody, psalmody, and instrumental and vocal soloists or ensembles is broader than what is found in the appendix. It is essential that you consult the parish staff about the music possibilities for the parish where the funeral will be.

It is important that appropriate music be chosen for liturgies. The parameters that limit the kinds of music appropriate to funerals are broad enough to accommodate individuality yet narrow enough to emphasize the equality of membership in the Body of Christ, the Church.[20]

In addition to particular parish musicians, you may, in consultation with the parish, have the option of requesting that friends or relatives who are trained as liturgical musicians take part in the liturgies.[21]

> I / We request the following musician(s) for the funeral vigil or principal funeral liturgy: _____
>
> _____
>
> _____
>
> _____ I / We would like the parish to select all musicians.

"Music . . . has the power to console and uplift the mourners and to strengthen the unity of the assembly in faith and love. The texts of the songs chosen for a particular celebration should express the paschal mystery of the Lord's suffering, death, and triumph over death and should be related to the readings from Scripture" (*OCF* §30).

---

[20] See Galatians 3:28; Romans 12:4-5; and Ephesians 5:23.
[21] In some instances a family may remain responsible for compensating parish musicians, whether or not they provide music at the funeral vigil or main liturgy, because of parish contracts with the musicians or for consultation services. A funeral home or parish staff member can advise you about this.

> _____ I / We suggest that the following music be considered for use at the funeral vigil or principal funeral liturgy: _____
>
> _____
> _____
> _____
> _____
> _____
>
> _____ I / We would like the parish to decide the matter of music.

19. Remembrance of the Deceased

Although it is not required, according to the *Order of Christian Funerals,* "A member or a friend of the family may speak in remembrance of the deceased before the final commendation begins."[22] Such a remembrance may also be given at the funeral vigil.[23]

In addition to the place of the funeral vigil, a remembrance of the deceased may also be given either in the church building or at the place of committal. Sometimes inclement weather or parish custom determines that the final commendation take place in the church building; if so, the remembrance of the deceased is given following the prayer after Communion[24] or after the Lord's Prayer.[25]

A remembrance of the deceased is a way to remember a person within the context of faith. When asking someone to offer a remembrance (or if someone has expressed an interest in this to you), please share the content guidelines for giving a remembrance of the deceased with that person (see appendix 5). You may want to give a copy of the completed "Information about the Deceased" form on pages 3–4 (and repeated on pages 43–44) to anyone who will share a remembrance. A person giving a remembrance may wish to consult with the homilist(s) or anyone else giving a remembrance so that the sharing is not too repetitive.

---

[22] *OCF* §§170 and 197.
[23] *OCF* §§62 and 366.
[24] *OCF* §§197 and 308.
[25] *OCF* §§195 and 308. This is the case, outside Mass, when there is no distribution of Holy Communion.

> I / We request that a remembrance of the deceased be given at the funeral vigil by: _____
> _____
>
> I / We request that a remembrance of the deceased be given at the principal funeral liturgy by: _____
> _____
>
> If possible, I / we would like the remembrance of the deceased at the principal funeral liturgy to be given:
>
> _____ during the liturgy (usually in a parish church or chapel).
>
> _____ at the place of committal (usually a cemetery).

In a less formal way, at the funeral vigil or afterwards, the assembly might be invited to share memories, stories, or "letters to the deceased." Both the young and old might find this inviting and helpful. If you are drawn to this idea, you can mention it to a parish staff member.

> _____ At or after the funeral vigil, I/we would like a general invitation to be extended to anyone present to share memories, stories, and thoughts about the deceased.

20. Rite of Committal

The time of committal is often difficult for family members as they "take leave"[26] of the body of their loved one. At the place of committal—often the place of other family graves—one who grieves seeks comfort and consolation; one hopes that loved ones rest in peace until the Lord's return in glory. A cemetery is a sacred resting place and the graves and other places of reposition are honored on account of the bodily or cremated remains that are present.

In the typical case of burial, the Catholic funeral liturgy allows for the coffin to be lowered into the ground while friends and

The rite of committal, "may be celebrated at the grave, tomb, or crematorium, and may be used for burial at sea" (OCF §204).

---

[26] *OCF* §218.

family are still present. If this is preferred it is important that the funeral home staff, as well as the presiding minister, know this preference.

> _____ I / We would like the family and friends to be present during the lowering of the coffin.
>
> _____ I / We would like only the family to be present during the lowering of the coffin.
>
> _____ I / We do not want to be present during the lowering of the coffin.

Such customs as tossing handfuls of dirt or flowers into the grave ritualizes participation in the burial and a sense of finality for family members at this time.

> _____ I / We would like family members and friends to be able to place flowers in the grave.
>
> _____ I / We would like family member to be able to toss dirt into the grave.
>
> _____ The family does not wish to exercise these options.
>
> Notes: _____
> _____

21. Memorabilia

Apart from the liturgical rituals provided by the *Order of Christian Funerals,* in order to make the funeral more personal, you may want to discuss with the funeral home staff and parish staff different ways of making the days of ritual and grieving more personal. For example, a funeral home setting may be enhanced with photographs, remembrances, and even special objects which were significant in the deceased's life. It is appropriate during the time of visitation that the deceased's life be remembered.

In some instances families want to construct or display a collage of photographs and articles (published or personal) about the deceased, to be displayed during the hours of visitation. What the deceased wrote, made with his or her own hands, or enjoyed as a hobby might be displayed. The days of immediate grieving are a time for the family to be creative in remembering the role and significance of a loved person in their lives and in the lives of the deceased person's parish and community. It is a good to consult the funeral home staff and the parish staff if you have any ideas that may need their assistance, such as the need of a display board or table.

There is no obligation to do any particular thing, and some families prefer to rely solely on the rituals themselves and the presence of friends and relatives.

Notes regarding memorabilia: _____
_____
_____

22. Gathering in the Presence of the Body

The Church provides an adaptable rite which is "a model of prayer that may be used when the family first gathers in the presence of the body, when the body is to be prepared for burial, or after it has been prepared. The family members, in assembling in the presence of the body, confront in the most immediate way the fact of their loss and the mystery of death."[27] This rite may be led by either an ordained or lay minister. If neither an ordained nor lay minister is available to lead this rite, a family member or funeral home staff member may choose to lead a prayer from this rite. One is found on page 25 of this booklet.

23. Transfer of the Body to the Church or to the Place of Committal

The *Order of Christian Funerals* provides a rite of transfer "to be used for prayer with the family and close friends as they prepare to accompany the body of the deceased in procession to the church or to the place of committal."[28] If a minister is unable to be present (for example, when the body is transferred from a funeral home to the parish church), a family member or funeral home staff member may choose to lead prayers. Two prayers drawn from the rite are found on page 25 of this booklet.

---

[27] *OCF* §109.
[28] *OCF* §119.

24. Refreshments and Luncheon

For the period of visitation in a funeral home, typically a room for family to rest away from visitors and perhaps to snack is provided. Consult with the funeral home staff as to what is provided for refreshments and what you may wish to provide on your own.

Many parishes provide a luncheon or refreshments after a funeral. You will want to check the possibilities with a parish staff member if you wish to provide refreshments for those present at a funeral, before they return to their homes.

Notes regarding refreshments: _____

_____

_____

_____

_____

_____

Conclusion

"We do not want you to be unaware . . . about those who have fallen asleep, so that you may not grieve like the rest, who have no hope. For if we believe that Jesus died and rose, so too will God, through Jesus, bring with him those who have fallen asleep" (1 Thessalonians 4:13-14).

We have described the roles of those who minister during the funeral journey as well as other concerns. All of these play a role in helping us "say goodbye" in a faith-filled, spiritual way. Liturgy invites everyone to be prepared to celebrate in a prayerful and meaningful way the life of the deceased within the context of faith and hope in Christ. It is a time to express grief and sadness, yet the sadness is not like the sadness of those who do not have hope (see 1 Thessalonians 4:13). The celebration of funeral rites brings comfort and consolation.

The rituals of the Church are expressions of our hope for those who have died and for those of us who remain and await our call to eternal life.

Prayers

Prayer at the Time of Gathering in the Presence of the Body

Into your hands, O Lord,
we humbly entrust our brother/sister N.
In this life you embraced him/her with tender love;
deliver him/her now from every evil
and bid him/her enter eternal rest.

The old order has passed away
welcome him/her then into paradise,
where there will be no sorrow, no weeping nor pain,
but the fullness of peace and joy
with your Son and the Holy Spirit
for ever and ever.

℟. Amen.[29]

Prayers at the Time of Transfer of the Body to the Church or to the Place of Committal

God of all consolation,
open our hearts to your word,
so that, listening to it, we may comfort one another,
finding light in time of darkness
and faith in time of doubt.

We ask this through Christ our Lord.

℟. Amen.[30]

May the Lord guard our going in and our going out.
May God be with us today
as we make this last journey with our brother/sister.[31]

---

[29] *OCF* §117.
[30] *OCF* §125.
[31] *OCF* §126.

Appendix 1
OPTIONS FOR THE FUNERAL VIGIL

Option 1	*Option 2*	*Option 3*
Vigil for the Deceased	**Vigil for the Deceased with Reception at the Church**	**Evening Prayer—Office for the Dead from the Liturgy of the Hours**
INTRODUCTORY RITES 　Greeting 　Opening Song 　Invitation to Prayer 　Opening Prayer	INTRODUCTORY RITES 　Greeting 　Sprinkling with Holy Water 　Placing of the Pall (optional) 　Entrance Procession (with song) 　Placing of Christian Symbols (optional) 　Invitation to Prayer 　Opening Prayer	INTRODUCTORY RITES 　Opening Verse and Hymn or Reception of the Body: 　　Greeting 　　Sprinkling with Holy Water 　　Placing of the Pall (optional) 　　Entrance Procession (with song) 　　Placing of Christian Symbols (optional) 　　Invitation to Prayer 　　Opening Prayer
LITURGY OF THE WORD 　First Reading 　Responsorial Psalm 　Gospel 　Homily	LITURGY OF THE WORD 　First Reading 　Responsorial Psalm 　Gospel 　Homily	PSALMODY READING(S) 　First Reading (biblical) 　Second Reading (optional, nonbiblical) HOMILY (optional)
PRAYER OF INTERCESSION 　Litany 　The Lord's Prayer 　Concluding Prayer 　Remembrance of the Deceased (optional)	PRAYER OF INTERCESSION 　Litany 　The Lord's Prayer 　Concluding Prayer 　Remembrance of the Deceased (optional)	PRAYER OF INTERCESSION
CONCLUDING RITE 　Blessing	CONCLUDING RITE 　Blessing	CONCLUDING RITE 　Concluding Prayer 　Remembrance of the Deceased (optional) 　Dismissal

Appendix 2
OPTIONS FOR FUNERAL AND RITE OF COMMITTAL

Funeral Mass Outline
INTRODUCTORY RITES
  Greeting
  Sprinkling with Holy Water
  Placing of the Pall (optional)
  Entrance Procession
  Placing of Christian Symbols (optional)
  Invitation to Prayer
  Opening Prayer
LITURGY OF THE WORD
  Readings
  Homily
  General Intercessions
    [Prayer of the Faithful]
LITURGY OF THE EUCHARIST
FINAL COMMENDATION[32]
  Invitation to Prayer
  Silence
  Signs of Farewell
    (optional; typically incense is used here)
  Song of Farewell
  Prayer of Commendation
PROCESSION TO THE PLACE OF COMMITTAL

Funeral outside Mass Outline
INTRODUCTORY RITES
  Greeting
  Sprinkling with Holy Water
  Placing of the Pall (optional)
  Entrance Procession
  Placing of Christian Symbols (optional)
  Opening Prayer
LITURGY OF THE WORD
  Readings
  Homily
  General Intercessions
    [Prayer of the Faithful]
  The Lord's Prayer
FINAL COMMENDATION[33]
  Invitation to Prayer
  Silence
  Signs of Farewell
    (optional; typically incense is used here)
  Song of Farewell
  Prayer of Commendation
PROCESSION TO THE PLACE OF COMMITTAL

Rite of Committal Outlines[34]

"The rite of committal is an expression of the communion that exists between the Church on earth and the Church in heaven" (OCF §206).

Option 1
Rite of Committal

Invitation
Scripture Verse
Prayer over the Place
  of Committal

Committal
Intercessions
The Lord's Prayer
Concluding Prayer

Prayer over the People

Option 2
Rite of Committal with Final Commendation

Invitation
Scripture Verse
Prayer over the Place
  of Committal

Invitation to Prayer
Silence
Signs of Farewell (optional;
  typically incense is used)
Song of Farewell
Prayer of Commendation
Committal

Prayer over the People

---

[32] This may take place at the place of committal (*OCF* §169).

[33] This may take place at the place of committal (*OCF* §196).

[34] The final commendation may take place before arriving at the place of committal, in which case option 1 is necessarily used for the committal (*OCF* §§169 and 196).

Appendix 3
SCRIPTURE SELECTION GUIDE

"As a general rule, all corresponding texts from sacred Scripture in the funeral rites are interchangeable. In consultation with the family and their close friends, the minister chooses texts that most clearly reflect the particular circumstances and the needs of the mourners" (*OCF* §344).

A parish staff member can show you these texts from *OCF* §§343–47.

You may use these Scripture summary lines and psalm antiphons to assist in the selection of Scripture texts for the funeral rites. You may also wish to use these Scripture summary lines and psalm antiphons for personal reflection.[35]

Funerals and Masses for the Dead

Reading I from the Old Testament

2 Maccabees 12:43-46	He acted in an excellent and noble way as he had the resurrection of the dead in view
Job 19:1, 23-27a	I know that my Vindicator lives.
Wisdom 3:1-9	As sacrificial offerings he took them to himself.
Wisdom 3:1-6, 9	As sacrificial offerings he took them to himself.
Wisdom 4:7-15	An unsullied life, the attainment of old age.
Isaiah 25:6a, 7-9	He will destroy death forever.
Lamentations 3:17-26	It is good to hope in silence for the saving help of the Lord.
Daniel 12:1-3	Many of those who sleep in the dust of the earth shall awake.

Reading I from the New Testament during the Season of Easter

Acts 10:34-43	He is the one appointed by God as judge of the living and the dead.
Acts 10:34-36, 42-43	He is the one appointed by God as judge of the living and the dead.
Revelation 14:13	Blessed are the dead who die in the Lord.
Revelation 20:11–21:1	The dead were judged according to their deeds.
Revelation 21:1-5a, 6b-7	There shall be no more death.

Responsorial Psalm

Psalm 23	The Lord is my shepherd; there is nothing I shall want.
Psalm 23	Though I walk in the valley of darkness, I fear no evil, for you are with me.
Psalm 25	To you, O Lord, I lift my soul.
Psalm 25	No one who waits for you, O Lord, will ever be put to shame.
Psalm 27	The Lord is my light and my salvation.
Psalm 27	I believe that I shall see the good things of the Lord in the land of the living.

---

[35] A parish staff member can show you the full text of these readings and psalm texts. Except where noted, selections are from the *Lectionary for Mass* (2001). The *Order of Christian Funerals*, §§343–47, may also be of assistance.

Psalms 42 and 43	My soul is thirsting for the living God: when shall I see him face to face?
Psalm 63	My soul is thirsting for you, O Lord, my God.
Psalm 103	The Lord is kind and merciful.
Psalm 103	The salvation of the just comes from the Lord.
Psalm 116	I will walk in the presence of the Lord in the land of the living.
Psalm 116	Alleluia.
Psalm 122	I rejoiced when I heard them say: let us go to the house of the Lord.
Psalm 122	Let us go rejoicing to the house of the Lord.
Psalm 130	Out of the depths, I cry to you, Lord.
Psalm 130	I hope in the Lord, I trust in his word.
Psalm 143	O Lord, hear my prayer.

Reading II from the New Testament

Romans 5:5-11	Since we are now justified by his Blood, we will be saved through him from the wrath.
Romans 5:17-21	Where sin increased, grace overflowed all the more.
Romans 6:3-9	We too might live in newness of life.
Romans 6:3-4, 8-9	We too might live in newness of life.
Romans 8:14-23	We also groan within ourselves as we wait for adoption, the redemption of our bodies.
Romans 8:31b-35, 37-39	What will separate us from the love of Christ?
Romans 14:7-9,10c-12	Whether we live or die, we are the Lord's.
1 Corinthians 15:20-28	So too in Christ shall all be brought to life.
1 Corinthians 15:20-23	So too in Christ shall all be brought to life.
1 Corinthians 15:51-57	Death is swallowed up in victory.
2 Corinthians 4:14–5:1	What is seen is transitory, but what is unseen is eternal.
2 Corinthians 5:1, 6-10	We have a building form God, eternal in heaven.
Philippians 3:20-21	He will change our lowly bodies to conform to his glory.
1 Thessalonians 4:13-18	Thus we shall always be with the Lord.
2 Timothy 2:8-13	If we have died with him we shall also live with him.
1 John 3:1-2	We shall see him as he is.
1 John 3:14-16	We know that we have passed from death to life because we love our brothers.

Gospel

Matthew 5:1-12a	Rejoice and be glad, for your reward will be great in heaven.
Matthew 11:25-30	Come to me and I will give you rest.
Matthew 25:1-13	Behold the bridegroom! Come out to him!

Matthew 25:31-46	Come, you who are blessed by my Father.
Mark 15:33-39; 16:1-6	Jesus gave a loud cry and breathed his last.
Mark 15:33-39	Jesus gave a loud cry and breathed his last.
Luke 7:11-17	Young man, I tell you, arise!
Luke 12:35-40	You also must be prepared.
Luke 23:33, 39-43	Today you will be with me in Paradise.
Luke 23:44-46, 50, 52-53; 24:1-6a	Father, into your hands I commend my spirit.
Luke 23:44-46, 50, 52-53	Father, into your hands I commend my spirit.
Luke 24:13-35	Was it not necessary that the Christ should suffer these things and enter into his glory?
Luke 24:13-16, 28-35	Was it not necessary that the Christ should suffer these things and enter into his glory?
John 5:24-29	Whoever hears my word and believes has passed from death to life.
John 6:37-40	Everyone who sees the Son and believes in him may have eternal life and I shall raise him on the last day.
John 6:51-59	Whoever eats this bread will live forever, and I will raise them up on the last day.
John 11:17-27	I am the resurrection and the life.
John 11:21-27	I am the resurrection and the life.
John 11:32-45	Lazarus, come out!
John 12:23-28	If it dies, it produces much fruit.
John 12:23-26	If it dies, it produces much fruit.
John 14:1-6	In my Father's house there are many dwellings.
John 17:24-26	I wish that where I am they also may be with me.
John 19:17-18, 25-39	And bowing his head he handed over his Spirit.

Funerals for Baptized Children

Reading I from the Old Testament

Isaiah 25:6a, 7-9	He will destroy death forever.
Lamentation 3:22-26	It is good to hope in silence for the saving help of the LORD.

Reading I from the New Testament during the Season of Easter

Revelation 7:9-10, 15-17	God will wipe every tear from their eyes.
Revelation 21:1a, 3-5a	There shall be no more death.

Responsorial Psalm

Psalm 23	The Lord is my shepherd; there is nothing I shall want.

Psalm 25	To you, O Lord, I lift up my soul.
Psalms 42 and 43	My soul is thirsting for the living God: when shall I see him face to face?
Psalm 148	Let all praise the name of the Lord.
Psalm 148	Alleluia.

Reading II from the New Testament

Romans 6:3-4, 8-9	We believe that we shall also live with him.
Romans 14:7-9	Whether we live or die, we are the Lord's.
1 Corinthians 15:20-23	So too in Christ shall all be brought to life.
Ephesians 1:3-5	He chose us in him, before the foundation of the world, to be holy.
1 Thessalonians 4:13-14, 18	We shall be with the Lord forever.

Gospel

Matthew 11:25-30	You have hidden these things from the wise and the learned and have revealed them to the childlike.
Mark 10:13-16	The Kingdom of heaven belongs to little children.
John 6:37-40	This is the will of my Father, that I should not lose anything of what he gave me.
John 6:37-39	This is the will of my Father, that I should not lose anything of what he gave me.
John 6:51-58	Whoever eats this bread will live forever, and I will raise him up on the last day. *(For a child who had already received the Eucharist)*
John 11:32-38, 40	If you believe, you will see the glory of God.
John 19:25-30	Behold, your mother.

Funerals for Children Who Died before Baptism

Reading I from the Old Testament

Isaiah 25:6a, 7-8	He will destroy death forever.
Lamentations 3:22-26	It is good to hope in silence for the saving help of the Lord.

Responsorial Psalm

Psalm 25	To you, O Lord, I lift up my soul.

Gospel

Matthew 11:25-30	You have hidden these things from the wise and the learned and have revealed them to the childlike.

Mark 15:33-46	Jesus gave a loud cry and breathed his last.
John 19:25-30	Behold, your mother.

Psalms and Antiphons That May Be Used in Various Places in the Funeral Rites[36]

Psalm 23	Remember me in your kingdom, Lord.
Psalm 25	Look on my grief and my sorrow: forgive all my sins.
	May the angels lead you into paradise; may the martyrs come to welcome you and take you to the holy city, the new and eternal Jerusalem.
Psalm 42	I will go to the dwelling of God, to the wonderful house of my Savior.
Psalm 51	Eternal rest, O Lord, and your perpetual light.
	Caught up with Christ, rejoice with the saints in glory.
	The bones that were broken shall leap for joy.
Psalm 93	From clay you shaped me; with flesh you clothed me;
	Redeemer, raise me on the last day.
Psalms 114 and 115:1-12	May Christ welcome you into paradise.
Psalms 114 and 115:1-12	Alleluia.
Psalm 116	May choirs of angels welcome you and lead you to the bosom of Abraham. May you find eternal rest where Lazarus is poor no longer.
Psalm 116	I heard a voice from heaven: Blessed are those who die in the Lord.
Psalm 116	Alleluia.
Psalm 118	Open for me the holy gates; I will enter and praise the Lord.
Psalm 118	This is the gate of the Lord: here the just shall enter.
Psalm 119:1-8	They are happy who live by the law of God.[37]
Psalm 119:9-16	May you be for ever blessed, O Lord; teach me your holy ways.
Psalm 119:17-24	Open my eyes, O Lord, that I may see the wonders of your law.
Psalm 119:25-32	Lightly I run in the way you have shown, for you have opened my heart to receive your law.
Psalm 119:33-40	Lead me, Lord, in the path of your commands.
Psalm 119:41-48	Blessed are those who hear the word of God and cherish it in their hearts.

---

[36] The following material is from *OCF* §347. Certain words are capitalized differently than in the newer *Lectionary for Mass*.

[37] "This antiphon may serve as the common antiphon for Psalm 119 or an antiphon proper to each part of Psalm 119 may be used" (*OCF* §347).

Psalm 119:49-56	In the land of exile I have kept your commands.
Psalm 119:57-64	I have pondered my ways and turned back to your teaching.
Psalm 119:65-72	More precious that silver or gold is the law you teach, O Lord.
Psalm 119:73-80	Let your loyal love console me, as you promised your servant.
Psalm 119:81-88	Heaven and earth will pass away, but my words will not pass away.
Psalm 119:89-96	I have sought to do your will, O Lord; for this you give me life.
Psalm 119:97-104	Law finds its fulfillment in love.
	How sweet your promise, richer than honey from the comb.
Psalm 119:105-112	Whoever follows me will not walk in the dark, but will have the light of life.
Psalm 119:113-120	Receive me, Lord, as you promised, that I may live.
Psalm 119:121-128	Give your servant a loving welcome, O Lord.
Psalm 119:129-136	Guide my steps according to your promise, O Lord.
Psalm 119:137-144	Do the things you have learned, and you will be blessed.
Psalm 119:145-152	I cry for your help, O Lord; your word is my hope.
Psalm 119:153-160	If you love me, keep my commandments, says the Lord.
Psalm 119:161-168	Great is the peace of those who keep your law, O Lord.
Psalm 119:169-176	I have chosen to do you will; may your hand be always there to give me strength.
Psalm 121	My help is from the Lord who made heaven and earth.
Psalm 122	Let us go the house of the Lord.
Psalm 122	I rejoiced when I heard them say: let us go to the house of the Lord.
Psalm 123	Our eyes are fixed on the Lord, pleading for his mercy.
Psalm 123	To you, O Lord, I lift up my eyes.
Psalm 126	Those who sow in tears shall sing for joy when they reap.
Psalm 130	I cry to you, O Lord.
Psalm 130	My soul has hoped in the Lord.
Psalm 132	Let your holy people rejoice, O Lord, as they enter your dwelling place.
Psalm 134	Bless the Lord, all you servants of the Lord.
Psalm 134	In the stillness of the night, bless the Lord.

Appendix 4
MUSIC LIST

The following music is from worship aids published by the Liturgical Press.[38] The numbers in the left columns are from the bilingual booklet for funeral vigils; the numbers in the right columns are from the bilingual booklet for the principal funeral liturgy (Mass or outside of Mass).[39]

45	29	Acuérdate de Jesucristo	29	13	Lord of the Living
13	1	Amazing Grace	37		Lord, You Have the Words
46	35	Arriba los Corazones	28		Magnificat: Mary's Song
14	3	Be Not Afraid	43–48		Mass of Creation
15		Because the Lord Is My Shepherd		11	May Christ Console Your Grieving Heart
16	4	Blest Are They	39		Mi Alma Tiene Sed
53		Canto de María	49–54		Misa San José
43		Cerca Está el Señor	41		Muéstranos, Señor
	5	Come to His/Her Aid (Song of Farewell)		14	My Shepherd Will Supply My Need
	27	Como Busca la Cierva	8	15	My Soul Is Thirsting
	39	Concédeles el Descanso Eterno	30		Now the Green Blade Rises
	30	Cristo, Recuérdame		16	O Lord, You Died That All Might Live
44	37	Cristo Vence	31	18	On Eagle's Wings
52	38	Dale el Descanso, Señor	49	40	Oye el Llamado
17		Day Is Done		31	Pan de Vida
40		Dichosos los que Viven	36		Protégeme, Dios Mío
	2	Eat This Bread	36		Que los Ángeles Te Lleven al Paraíso
42		El Señor es Compasivo	47	41	Quién Es Ese
38		El Señor Es Mi Luz		42	Quiero Ser, Señor, Instrumento de Tu Paz
18		Enfold Me in Your Love			
19		Eye Has Not Seen	32		Resucitó
	8	Gift of Finest Wheat	25		Saints of God
20	7	God of Love		34	Señor, Mi Dios
	32	He Is Risen	37		Señor, Tú Tienes Palabras
21		Holy Darkness	1		Shelter Me, O God
	34	How Great Thou Art	2	17	Shepherd Me, O God
12	22	How Lovely Is Your Dwelling Place	41		Show Us, O Lord
	33	I Am the Bread of Life	32	24	Stand Firm in Faith
22	9	I Call You to My Father's House	7		The Cry of the Poor
	23	I Heard the Voice of Jesus Say		6	The Hand of God Shall Hold You
23	12	I Know That My Redeemer Lives	26		The King Shall Come
24		In the Lord Is My Joy	4		The Lord Is My Light (Haas)
	10	Jerusalem, My Destiny	5	20	The Lord Is My Light (Willcock)
25		Jerusalem, My Happy Home	38		The Lord Is My Light (Hurd)
50		Jesús, el Buen Pastor	3	19	The Lord Is My Shepherd
	30	Jesus, Remember Me	43		The Lord Is Near
45	29	Keep in Mind	42		The Lord Is Rich in Kindness
36		Keep Me Safe, O God	48	28	The Strife Is O'er
51		La Muerte No Es el Final	33	26	We Offer Prayer in Sorrow, Lord
48	28	La Ruda Lucha Terminó	34		We Thank You, Father, Lord of All
54		Las Puertas de la Nueva Ciudad		33	Yo Soy el Pan de Vida
	27	Like a Deer	35		You Are Mine
6	21	Like the Deer That Longs	11		You Are Near
9		Like the Deer That Yearns	10		Your Love Is Finer Than Life
	27	Lord of All Hopefulness			

---

[38] This music is also available from other publishers. Other sacred music is also possible.

[39] The numbers are different in the single accompaniment book that serves both booklets.

Appendix 5

GIVING A REMEMBRANCE OF THE DECEASED

These guidelines are intended as helps for anyone who is asked to give a remembrance of the deceased at a funeral vigil, funeral proper (at or outside Mass) or at a committal. It is important for the person giving the remembrance to be sensitive to the liturgical tone set by the ritual and worship space. Particular parishes and dioceses may also have guidelines or suggestions, so it is best to check with a parish staff member to see if such exist.

1. You have to be aware of your own limitations. While it is an honor to be asked to give a reflection you may decline. It may be that the task is too emotional or difficult. Everyone will respect your decision if you wish to decline the invitation. You may want to ask someone (who is willing and able) to be willing to "step in" for you in case you cannot complete your remarks. See also number 2, below.

2. It is a good idea to have the text of the remembrance on the lectern or ambo from which the remembrance will be presented.

3. A remembrance of the deceased is a way of placing the life of the deceased and the present experience of loss within the context of faith. How was the deceased's life an imitation of Christ? How was he/she a person of sharing (healing, helping, feeding, building, teaching, etc.)?

4. It is best not to idealize the life of the deceased.

5. It is important not to speak at great length. You might ask a parish staff member if there are local restrictions on length, for example, three to five minutes.

6. There are definite religious/theological themes that permeate funerals. These are evident in the readings from Scripture. What can be said about how God worked in the life of the deceased? How did the deceased share a unique, holy life with family, friends, church, and world?

7. An important purpose of the reflection is to give needed support to family members and friends. The remarks should directly or indirectly give comfort to those who grieve and not draw an undue amount of attention to yourself.

8. The remembrance is an opportunity to deepen the assembly's faith. What can be said about the deceased that helps or encourages the assembly?

9. It is best to communicate in your own style. While humor is possible and even healing, it must be done carefully and in good taste.

10. It is a good idea to have a parish staff member or someone else whom you respect read over and critique your presentation.

11. Please know that what is most important to those who grieve is your presence and your connection with them and/or the deceased.

12. Last but not least, keep in mind that you are participating in the sacred funeral rites of a relative or friend. Pray for guidance from the Holy Spirit, "the Comforter" for yourself and for the assembly.

Summary of Requests and Information

Section 1. Funeral Home and Parish

I / We would like this funeral home to handle the funeral arrangements:
_____

I / We would like this parish church to handle the liturgical arrangements for the funeral:
_____

Section 2. Committal and Disposition of the Body of the Deceased

For this funeral, I / we would like:

_____ a traditional burial.

    At this cemetery: _____

    On this date: _____

    At this time: _____

(This is often following the funeral, but circumstances may prevent this.)

_____ cremation to occur before the funeral liturgy.

_____ cremation to occur after the funeral liturgy.

    I / We would like the committal of the ashes to take place:

    At this place: _____

    On this date: _____

    At this time: _____

Special circumstances: _____
_____
_____

Section 3. Scheduling the Principal Funeral Liturgy

I / We would like

_____ the principal funeral liturgy within the eucharistic celebration of a Mass.

    I / We would like the Mass to be celebrated

        _____ in the parish church.

        at _____, with the approval of the parish staff.

    (The place might be a recognized chapel within a parish.)

I / We would like:

_____ the principal funeral liturgy to be celebrated apart from a Mass.

    I / We would like the celebration to take place at:

    _____

    I / We would like this to be:

        _____ with the distribution of Holy Communion.

        _____ without the distribution of Holy Communion.

I / We would like the principal funeral liturgy to take place on this day at this time:
_____

Section 4. Scheduling the Funeral Vigil

I / We would like the funeral vigil to take place:

    At this place: _____

    At this time: _____

    On this date: _____

Section 5. Visitation

I / We would like there to be public visitation on these days (or this day) and at these hours: _____
_____

I / We would like there to be private visitation on this day at this time: _____
_____

The place(s) of visitation is (are): _____
_____

Notes concerning the clothing and the preparation of the body of the deceased:
_____
_____

Section 6. Leaders/Presiders

If possible, I / we would like this (these) minister(s) to be involved in leading services:

At the vigil: _____

At the funeral liturgy: _____

At the committal: _____

    _____ I / We would like the parish staff to decide the matters of who is to preside and when.

Section 7. Funeral Vigil

_____ I / We would like to do what is customary in regard to the format of the vigil.

_____ I / We would like to discuss the format options for the funeral vigil with a parish staff member.

I / We would like the reception of the body to take place:

_____ at the funeral vigil.

_____ at the funeral Mass or liturgy.

_____ I / We would like the parish staff to decide the matter of when the body is to be received.

_____ I / We would like to have the rosary prayed publicly during the time of visitation.

We would like the rosary to be led by _____

at this time _____ on this day _____

_____ I / We would prefer not to have the rosary prayed publicly during the time of visitation.

_____ I / We would like the parish staff to decide the matter of praying the rosary or not.

Section 8. Pallbearers

I / We would like the following persons to be pallbearers for the funeral: _____

_____

_____

_____

_____

_____ I / We would like the parish staff to decide the matter of pallbearers.

Section 9. Placing of the Pall

The family designates the following people for the unfolding and placing of the pall on the coffin at the entrance of the church: _____

_____

_____

_____ I / We would the parish staff to decide the matter of who will place pall.

Section 10. Placing of Christian Symbols

We would like to place the following Christian symbol on the coffin: _____
_____

The person(s) designated to place the Christian symbol(s) is (are): _____
_____

_____ I / We would like the parish staff to decide the matter of additional Christian symbols.

Section 11. Server(s)

I / We request that the following person(s) be server(s) for the funeral vigil: _____
_____
_____

I / We request that the following person(s) be server(s) for the principal funeral liturgy:
_____
_____

_____ I / We would like the parish staff to decide the matter of the servers will be.

Section 12. Lector(s)

I / We request that the following person(s) be lector(s) for the funeral vigil:

For the first reading: _____

For the responsorial psalm or responsory (if not sung): _____

For the second reading (if there is one): _____
_____

The Gospel is to be read by: _____

_____ I / We would like the parish staff to decide the matter of who the lectors will be at the funeral vigil.

I / We request that the following person(s) be lector(s) for the principal funeral liturgy:

For the first reading: _____

For the responsorial psalm (if not sung): _____

For the second reading (if there is one): _____

The Gospel is to be read by: _____

_____ I / We would like the parish staff to decide the matter of who the lectors will be at the principal funeral liturgy.

Section 13. Readings

I / We request that the following readings be proclaimed at the funeral vigil:

The first reading: _____

The responsorial psalm or responsory (if not sung): _____

The second reading (if there is one): _____

The Gospel: _____

    _____ I / We would like the parish staff to decide the matter of readings for the funeral vigil.

I / We request that the following readings be proclaimed at the principal funeral liturgy:

The first reading: _____

The responsorial psalm (if not sung): _____

The second reading (if there is one): _____

The Gospel: _____

    _____ I / We would like the parish staff to decide the matter of readings for the principal funeral liturgy.

Section 14. Homilies

See section 14 in the text.

Section 15. Prayer of the Faithful

I / We would like to have the names of the following deceased persons and the following concerns to be mentioned in prayer as part of the intercessions of the funeral liturgy: _____

_____

_____

_____

    _____ I / We would like the parish staff to decide the matter of the content of the intercessions.

I / We request that the following person proclaim the intercessions at the principal funeral liturgy: _____

    _____ I / We would like the parish staff to decide the matter of who will proclaim the intercessions.

Section 16. Preparation of the Gifts at Mass

I / We request that the following persons bring the gifts forward: _____

_____

Section 17. Ministers of Holy Communion

I / We would like the following person(s) to assist in the distribution of Holy Communion:

_____

_____

_____ I / We would like the parish staff to decide the matter of who will distribute Holy Commuunion.

Section 18. Music

I / We request the following musician(s) for the funeral vigil or principal funeral liturgy:

_____

_____

_____ I / We would like the parish to select all musicians.

I / We suggest that the following music be considered for use at the funeral vigil or principal funeral liturgy: _____

_____

_____

_____

_____

_____ I / We would like the parish to decide the matter of music.

Section 19: Remembrance of the Deceased

I / We request that a remembrance of the deceased be given at the funeral vigil by

_____

I / We request that a remembrance of the deceased be given at the principal funeral liturgy by: _____

If possible I / we would like the at the principal funeral liturgy to be given

_____ during the liturgy (usually in a parish church or chapel).

_____ at the place of committal (usually a cemetery).

_____ at or after the funeral vigil, I/we would like a general invitation to be extended to anyone present to share memories, stories, and thoughts about the deceased.

Section 20. Rite of Committal

_____ I / We would like the family and friends to be present during the lowering of the coffin.

_____ I / We would like only the family to be present during the lowering of the coffin.

_____ I / We do not want to be present during the lowering of the coffin.

_____ I / We would like family members and friends to be able to place flowers in the grave.

_____ I / We would like family member to be able to toss dirt into the grave.

_____ The family does not wish to exercise these options.

Notes: _____

Section 21. Memorabilia

Notes regarding memorabilia: _____

_____
_____
_____
_____

Sections 22 and 23. Gathering in the Presence of the Body / Transfer of the Body

See the prayers on page 25.

Section 24. Refreshments and Luncheon

Notes regarding refreshments and luncheon: _____

_____
_____
_____
_____
_____
_____

Information about the Deceased (*The following is also found on pages 3–4.*)

Name of the deceased: _____

Nickname: _____

Name to be used in liturgical prayers: _____

Maiden name: _____

Age of the deceased: _____

Son/Daughter of: _____

_____

Surviving loved ones:

    Spouse: _____

    Children (names, places of residence, spouses): _____

    _____

    _____

    _____

    _____

    _____

    Grandchildren and great-grandchildren (names): _____

    _____

    _____

    _____

    _____

    Others of special note: _____

    _____

    _____

Place of birth: _____

Name of spouse (if deceased): _____

Date and place of marriage: _____

Residence history: _____

_____

_____

_____

Summary of Requests and Information

Education history: _____

_____

_____

_____

Work history: _____

_____

_____

_____

Special or ordinary accomplishments: _____

_____

_____

_____

Parish membership and service: _____

_____

_____

Membership in other organizations: _____

_____

_____

_____

Hobbies and recreational activities: _____

_____

_____

_____

Words or descriptions that characterized the deceased:

_____

_____

_____

Preceded in death by: _____

_____

_____